A Desk in the Elephant House

A Desk in the Elephant House

Cathryn Essinger

Texas Tech University Press

The Walt McDonald First-Book Poetry Series

© Copyright 1998 Texas Tech University Press

This book was set in Arrus BT and printed on acid-free paper
that meets the guidelines for permanence and durability of the
Committee on Production Guidelines for Book Longevity of
the Council on Library Resources.(∞)

Printed in the United States of America

Book and jacket design by Melissa Bartz

Library of Congress Cataloging-in-Publication Data

    Essinger, Cathryn, 1947-
      A desk in the elephant house / Cathryn Essinger.
        p. cm. — (Walt McDonald first-book poetry series)
      ISBN 0-89672-401-8
      I. Title. II. Series.
      PS3555.S683D47 1998
      811'.54—dc21   97-48560
                                            CIP

98 99 00 01 02 03 04 05 06 / 9 8 7 6 5 4 3 2 1

Texas Tech University Press
Box 41037
Lubbock, Texas 79409-1037 USA
800-832-4042
ttup@ttu.edu

Acknowledgments

I am grateful to the editors of the following publications in which
  a number of my poems, several in earlier verions, first appeared:
Buffalo Spree: "Talking to Flowers"
National Poetry Competition, Chester H. Jones Foundation:
  "Equinox"
Negative Capability: "The Mathematician, Counting"
Poetry: "For Six Friends," "Growing Accustomed to Green," "Not
  to Reply," "The Philosophy Professor Discusses the Nature of
  the Self-Consciousness Mind," "You Are Right"
Poetry Northwest: "English 123 Discusses Virginia Woolf"
Prize Poems: National Federation of State Poetry Societies: "Alice Reads
  to the Daffodils," "Green Will," "Patching the Sky,"
  "Running," "Two Apples"
Western Ohio Journal: "David"
Yankee: "Moon Garden," "To the Power of the Air"

I would like to thank my mother, Marjorie Schmid, for her many
  proof readings of this manuscript; the talented poets in my
  Writer's Group for whom the poem "Six Friends" was written;
  and Robert A. Fink and Judith Keeling at Texas Tech
  University Press for the kindness, enthusiasm and expertise
  that made this book possible.

Other Walt McDonald Winners

Foreword

Cathryn Essinger's book *A Desk in the Elephant House* is a brilliant, beautiful orchestration of sensuous, intellectual, witty, accessible poetry. Most of all, it is a symphony of stunning imagery. Ezra Pound defines the "Image" as "that which presents an intellectual and emotional complex in an instant of time." Pound explains that when the Image presents this complex instantaneously, it "gives the sense of sudden liberation; that sense of freedom from time limits and space limits; the sense of sudden growth, which we experience in the presence of the greatest works of art." *A Desk in the Elephant House* is a wonderfully wrought intellectual and emotional work of art, a work of philosophy, theology, psychology, botany—a composition of imagistic language transposing the concrete and the figurative, the mundane and the metaphysical. It's all the senses can do to keep up.

Emily Dickinson located poets "Exterior—to Time—." In the first two stanzas of her poem #448, she might have been anticipating Cathryn Essinger:

This was a Poet—It is That
Distills amazing sense
From ordinary Meanings—
And Attar so immense
From the familiar species . . ..

Like Dickinson, Essinger is teacher and student, doubter and believer, observer of the empirical world and intuitive *knower* of the metaphysical. She is immersed in reality while simultaneously questioning that reality. Her world is localized and wonderfully strange. The focus for this sensuously philosophical poet is how to know the "familiar."

Cathryn Essinger begins her book with a pair of epigraphs, each from Ralph Waldo Emerson's essay "The American Scholar." The first—"at the feet of the familiar"—is excerpted from "I embrace the common, I explore and sit at the feet of the familiar." The second epigraph asks, "What would we really know the meaning of? The meal in the firkin; the milk in the pan; the ballad in the street; the news of the boat." Emerson and Essinger demand "insight into to-day," desiring to know "the sublime presence of the highest spiritual cause lurking . . . in these suburbs and extremities of nature" ("The American Scholar").

How *can* we discern form and order in a familiar world paradoxical at best? We can rely on our empirical senses, but such knowledge is limited to what we see, hear, taste, touch, and smell. There is, however, another level of *knowing* that Emerson and Immanuel Kant called "intuition." In his essay "The Transcendentalist," Emerson

vii

agrees with Kant that "there was a very important class of ideas or imperative forms which did not come by experience, but through which experience was acquired; that these were intuitions of the mind itself . . .." As the art history professor declares in Cathryn Essinger's "Art History 121," "'Reality is a slippery subject.'" It is both as intrusive as the philosophy professor's "big and white, / loose-jointed, lumbering" polar bear squat in the middle of the classroom, and as invisible as the same bear against a field of white ("The Philosophy Professor Discusses the Nature of the Self-Conscious Mind or The Invisible Bear"). Reality is the familiar blue jay raucous as a crow, the blue jay we only *think* we see, since scientists have shown that "the blue jay must be invisible, / for blue is not blue, / but the absence of blue" ("As I Try To Explain, No Words Come Out"). Reality is often too familiar—the *truth we didn't tell* hanging "in another room where Noah plugs his ears / against the screams of the dying, / and elephants stand knee-deep in rain" ("Watercolor"). On the other hand, reality can be as comforting as women gathered "beside the fire" weaving "the truths and lies that make / them friends" ("For Six Friends"). It can be as stark as "the morning news . . . a drive-by / shooting and an old murder" ("Morning News: Three Stories That Deserve Better Telling") or as consoling as "the other side / of the day where everything is bright / and properly placed" ("Ropes and Ladders"), where a physical wasp can step "onto the invisible / staircase, and into the air. . . " ("English 123 Discusses Virginia Woolf"). Reality is slippery. Like the student David "who wrote furiously / on his exams, not because he did not know the answer, / but because he knew too many answers—" ("David"), we have lived too long with the paradoxical invisible-familiar elephants ("A Desk in the Elephant House"), polar bears, and blue jays to satisfy ourselves with only one definition of reality. No wonder the question of *A Desk in the Elephant House* is David's to his literature professor: "'How can you know? How can you possibly know?'" ("David").

The persona of Cathryn Essinger's book seems haunted by David's question. The persona is a poet, a college literature teacher, an art aficionado, a wife, a mother, a sister, a daughter, a friend, a gardener. She is engaged in the study of her familiar world. She knows "the stillness in an empty room" ("A Desk In The Elephant House") where, "with disbelief," she has sat "alone in the dark, wondering / what is left to bargain with" ("Eclipse") and whether or not "any god" loves us "enough to make the light return" ("Eclipse"). She discovers no "notes on the bedside table, no clues" ("Morning News: Three Stories That Deserve Better Telling"). She *wants* to explain to the toad that "trusts in divine intervention" ("Drought") that she does "not believe in the hand of fate, / or faith, or even in luck itself" ("Drought"), but the reality of her familiar morning encounter with the toad belly-flopped in the dog's water bowl is that

viii

the toad *does* get saved each morning, and *she* is his savior. How can she explain her disbelief when the toad follows her with his eyes, his thin lips tucked "so smoothly into the corners / of his cheeks" that she thinks he's smiling ("Drought")?

Because she would like to believe "in immortality— / that ultimate of thrifts" ("Letter To Jerry"), she does not despair. In a "winter space," she confirms *wonder* ("In a Winter Space"). When she caresses her dog, the persona recognizes the joy of an animal melting into a world where feeling becomes knowledge, thoughts sensations. The dog "accepts all forms of giving" ("Not Understanding Hands"). Given a choice, the persona will opt for Romance over Realism. In "Amniotic," she declares, "Still I want my bit of ignorance, / the amniotic mystery of corn." Looking close at the familiar, she finds mystery, and her new perspective causes "everything else" to appear "changed, wild and strange" ("Growing Accustomed to Green"). The persona does not conclude her study with an answer to David's question "How can you possibly know?" Rather, she seems to be celebrating the fact that she *can't* offer a definitive answer. She lives in a world running out of time, but each morning new life commences, and she awakens into the mystery, the surprise of another familiar day ("Ropes and Ladders").

The opening section consists of only the title poem. "A Desk In The Elephant House" introduces the persona's paradox—how to explain a reality so huge, so familiar, so metaphysical:

> Sometimes something huge sits down
>   beside you, and it is so large, so
> familiar, that even though you feel
>   its breath upon your cheek
> you are unaware of its presence.
>
> I have lived so long with the elephants
>   that I can no longer tell you
> when they come and when they go . . .
>   their huge bodies fill the room
> and yet they move so quietly, are so
>
> light on their wonderful feet
>   that they may as well be ghosts.

The poet-persona places her "face against their flanks" but is "no more aware of them than the lover who turns in his sleep." Now, at her desk, she must rely on memory to "define their absence," because the elephants are there and not there: "They are the stillness in an empty room, / the touch too familiar to be known." She has recorded "the trivia of memory," but these empirical details cannot explain the familiar. She must rely on insubstantial intuition to explain the mystery, the strangeness of her familiar world.

Section Two, "The Touch Too Familiar," explores the world in which the persona makes her living: the college classroom where she engages the intellectual pursuit of literature, history, and art. Art provides little comfort, is not studied exclusively for beauty, but to confirm that the reality of each of our worlds is that our lives are most often defined by pain and death. The persona's students, "less curious about art than anatomy," must go forth into a new "industrial era" and face not the "'tinted steam'" of art, but a harsher atmosphere. Art history brings this home to the students, even here in "the air / conditioned chill" of this classroom where they, and their instructor, "crouch, arms around" their "knees, jackets thrown like shawls over bare limbs" ("Art History 121"). "Fourth Position, Grand *Jete*" offers two perspectives on art as well as two perspectives on the nature of male-female relationships. The first is "as a shadow on the museum wall," a perspective of freedom and beauty as Degas' bronze dancer seems, from a distance, to move "with the grace of one who knows / that she is being watched, but doesn't care / for this moment belongs to her, not to the artist." Up close, however, we observe the "pinches," the "smudges" along her thigh, and we ask, "Who tilted your head, raised your cheekbones / with his thumbs, then left you here, for the sake of art, a diary of all the ways he has touched you?" In two "paintings by David, one is forever pushed / and pulled" ("In These Paintings By David . . ."). The deaths of Socrates and Marat, at first, "seem like a gentle settling into place." It is only later that "we see death sitting at the end of the bed." Later "we see the water tinged with Marat's / blood, the glint of the knife, the length of / the dark blade." Even the cozy world of paired animals in Peter Spier's *Noah's Ark* "is not a pretty story" ("Watercolor"). Our world does not fear destruction from a second Flood; ours is "a world half annihilated / by the wonders of modern science" ("On The Beach"). It comes as no surprise the persona-instructor has trouble translating her marginal notes to her writing students: "Who am I to question / the slippery logic of the literary mind?" ("In A Literary Voice"). No wonder she does not have a comfortable answer for her student David's taunt: "'How can you know? How can you possibly know?'" ("David"). Maybe the implication of this section's title is that *this* reality's familiar touch is too *painfully* familiar. The persona, however, does not despair. Her intuitive, Romantic *knowing* seems to save her: "If some misunderstanding / seems to make sense, there is no loss. / A new mental geography takes over." She tells herself that "found logic is certainly better / than none at all." For the persona, "'God waits . . . / in a little red wagon'" if we "want Him to'" ("In A Literary Voice"). The persona's polar bear in "The Philosophy Professor Discusses the Nature of the Self-Conscious Mind or

The Invisible Bear" is "big and white, / loose-jointed, lumbering over the ice flow of the page." Of course he "sprawled / casually in the middle of the floor like a family pet" as soon as the philosophy professor commanded, "'Please do not think about bears.'" Who wouldn't love the invisible, existential, wet-fur-pungent, "plush reality" of such a bear? "Kant, Kierkegaard, and Sartre all owned bears, / big, fat, slumbering creatures whose paws twitched / in their sleep." They contemplated "essence versus / existence among polar seals." Cathryn Essinger's bear almost knew "the answer to some question" before he snuzzled "between the pads of one fat paw." The persona "bought him a bed, checked his teeth, / paid the vet." The persona seems delighted to claim him. She has only to think of a name. She also perceives beauty and humor in the self-confident wasp who, "after checking her pockets / for stones, steps onto the invisible / staircase, and into the air. . ." ("English 123 Discusses Virginia Woolf"). Yes, this world is one in which we are "surrounded by everyday clothing, the pinch / of the streets, the confines of expectations," but like "Caillebotte's / reclining nude," we can remove our boots, lie back "in a moment of erotic solitude" ("Nude On A Couch"). Yes, time is running out on us, on our world, but soon the sun will illuminate the morning; "in a moment the begonias will become / famous," and despite the often painful consequences of a changing order—"some Warhol [who] has picked up his brush and is throwing / paint onto the windshield"—, we exist; this is our moment; "we have all come along for the ride" ("A Response to Critics").

"The Intimacy of Strangers," Section Three, focuses on the persona's relationships with family and friends. She seems to be suggesting in the title of this section that intimacy (love, communication) in a world defined by *loss* will always be limited to relationships between strangers, no matter how well they appear to know each other. In "Biography," the persona says she has been reading Virginia Woolf, "trying to understand the nature of loss." The world constantly reminds us we are vulnerable, "lost / on a familiar street," and we hear "'lions in the dark'" ("Lions").

Time is a constant in this familiar world, and time, we know only too well, is running out: we are "turning / the pages against the clock" ("Lions"), and only mathematicians seem to have the "guts," the "pizzaz," to keep "adding and subtracting," devoting their lives "to the count." "All the while, the heart's / little time bomb is busy" ("The Mathematician, Counting"). The persona would stop time, suspend the familiar "between what it is / and what it is becoming" ("Not To Reply"). She would reclaim the lost, the dying, the dead. Her neighborhood is peopled with personalities only *she* perceives: Gorbachev "at the grocery store / palming heads of lettuce," "Einstein weighing / coffee beans," "Solzhenitsyn / at Quality Farm and Fleet," Billy Jean King, Gloria Steinem, and most significantly—the persona's "neighbor, / Maggie Keller, on the Troy-Urbana Road." The persona smiles and waves; Maggie smiles back. Maggie "has been dead for over a year" ("'Are You My Angel?'"). The persona wants her neighbor back, like she wants to reclaim her good friend Jerry: "On the night that you died / I looked for you everywhere" ("Letter To Jerry"). She wants to reclaim her sons sliding out of her life ("From the Top of the Hill"). She needs to call back her young father ("I Don't Remember Taking This Picture"), her young brother ("For My Brother, Reading Over My Shoulder"). She wants to believe in infinity, immortality, if only so *she* can return to gently haunt her six close friends, women weaving the "truths and lies that make / them friends" ("For Six Friends").

Can she stop time, hold on to what is lost, "as if absence could become its own harvest" ("For My Brother, Reading Over My Shoulder")? She is realist enough to know she can't, so she chooses to freeze-frame a moment of love and mystery: Her god-like carpenter hammers on the barn roof "patching the sky / with scraps of scratchy black," while the persona waits in "sweet hay" beneath "the barn's high dome" for the carpenter to finish the job, slide open the heavy door, and "stand alone / with light clinging to your trousers / and dawn settling about your feet" ("Patching the Sky"). In another stop-time moment, her son, at "the crossroads," turns "toward home" concluding his three-mile run. The neighbor's chocolate Lab who has accompanied the boy is panting at his feet. The boy; the Lab; the boy's "plump, but loyal" stay-at-home dog; and the boy's mother rest in "the stillness of evening." This is the moment the mother will preserve:

> Around us is the stillness of evening,
> corn and mint, and in the pond
> a blue heron steps so lightly he leaves no ripple-
> only the memory of motion.
> For a moment we are timeless,
> you and me and the trusting dogs.
> There is only this road, this night
> and you are my son forever. ("Running")

The final section, "Growing Accustomed to Green," depicts the persona as gardener / Earth Mother; but the reality of decay and the need for light prevent this garden from becoming Eden Before The Fall, prevent the gardener from being so sure of her world, of what she sees, that she becomes complacent, dogmatic. Her uncertainty permits her to discover mystery in her garden; it allows for the joy of surprise. She is not *accustomed* to Green; she is *growing* accustomed.

The first poem in this section, "Growing Accustomed to Green," highlights our learning to see, our growing familiar with Nature and its camouflaged, invisible creatures—the mystery that is always present in our everyday lives:

> now that green is no longer
> an oddity, but the one charm
> that is always given,
>
> when you look away, into
> the splash of field and meadow
> doesn't everything else appear
>
> changed, wild and strange?

This question, of course, is rhetorical. She delights in perceiving her world as an infinite harvest: "Tomorrow there will be apples and pears, / bushels to fill . . . always / this rising up, this bringing down." "Always," she declares, "I am standing / at the foot of the ladder / where everything is passed down" ("Ladders").

Though she prefers to think only of harvest, the persona knows that violence "blooms on every street / corner" ("Alice Reads to the Daffodils"). Headlines "are worrisome / for those who come in ruffles," and even April, the season of re-birth, is tentative in a land "where the light is / so unpredictable." Still there is beauty: "Still, there is the urgency / of spring, the rustle / of moonlight on city streets." Still, there is the paradoxical "flash of bloom, / so quick / it is almost bloodless" ("Alice Reads to the Daffodils"). This is the "blossom end / of the universe where / everything lives and dies," where the persona sows seed "oblivious to earthly time," ever mindful that she has "set some clock to ticking," and one consequence will be "the puckered scar / where the umbilical lets go" ("Blue Lakes and Scarlet Runners"). Against loss and death, against the inevitable—"everything / planned out, everything spoken for / even before it has begun"—, the persona chooses "the fragile gestures made by flowers / and the single word spoken / by each blossom, mouth to mouth" ("Talking to Flowers"). She chooses to know her world intuitively and invites us to do the same

> so we can arrive, once again,
> every summer, at this place
> so familiar we forget
> that it exists. ("Amniotic")

Salvation will come if we choose to "look up" at Icarus, at the "wings" of maples twirling "downward in death" ("Double-Winged Achenes"). We watch "the flutter and fall, / hear the rustle of despair," not to remind ourselves of the inevitable, but to join the firemen bracing "themselves on the wet pavement, / arms and legs bent to accept / the coming weight." Like them, we fix our eyes on "a single form," not to watch Icarus, women, and children fall, but to catch them before they reach the pavement ("Double-Winged Achenes").

The persona cannot explain how she can "possibly know" ("David") that the invisible is perceivable and familiar. Often words catch in her throat ("Today the Starlings Are Listening to Brahms . . . "); "no song is seen / no light heard" ("As I Try To Explain, No Words Come Out"), but, like the toad basking in the dog's water bowl, the persona is learning to trust "in divine intervention" ("Drought") even though the realist in her does "not believe in the hand of fate, / or faith, or even in luck itself" ("Drought"). Like the toad, the baby in "Moon Garden" believes the persona is Adam, Eve, even God as the persona and the baby name "every color / in the garden." The baby "laughed and laughed . . . / he thought I had invented them." She is the "name giver," but the baby, paradoxically, gives *her* new life, and she can laugh with him "seeing how he had invented me."

We cannot avoid the darkness, the moon's eclipse. Often "we sit alone in the dark." We wonder "what is left to bargain with / and if any god loves us enough / to make the light return" ("Eclipse"). We do not, however, despair, because occasionally

> a crow paces
> his way across the lawn
> with such purpose
>
> we know
> he is on a mission
> from someplace unknown. ("Coincidence")

Occasionally "the pear tree blossoms / with such fragility / that we choose, on the spot," existentially, "to believe in almost anything / post magic, post science" ("Coincidence"). We have no choice but to confront the darkness of loss; "we name things no longer / here" ("Dry Creek Bed"). We live "here among this polished absence" ("Dry Creek Bed") in a cold world "eight below, twelve inches / of snow," but we choose "to see / the truth behind the illusion"; it is our good doubt that "holds us . . . , still / wondering, in this winter space" ("In a Winter Space").

Cathryn Essinger concludes *A Desk in the Elephant House* by affirming the middle world, our familiar position between the world of intellect and that of sensation ("Not Understanding Hands"). We are small creatures "digging skyward, pushing through the roots / of stars, chewing at the webbing of the universe" ("Ropes and Ladders"). Ours is a precarious adventure "as we grope / for a hold on some steep cliff, hearing / only the whimper of ropes and lines / and the swish of the wind." Time "tangles / about our feet." Then suddenly we "awaken on the other side / of the day." Here "everything is bright / and properly placed." Everything is "familiar, so much the same" ("Ropes and Ladders"). Light divides the darkness. We know our world, and it is not waste and void. It is good.

Robert A. Fink

Contents

Growing Accustomed To Green

For Brent and Quincy

At the feet of the familiar . . .

*What would we really know
the meaning of? The meal in
the firkin; the milk in the pan;
the ballad in the street;
the news of the boat.*

Ralph Waldo Emerson
The American Scholar, 1837

A Desk in the Elephant House

A Desk in the Elephant House

Sometimes something huge sits down
      beside you, and it is so large, so
familiar, that even though you feel
      its breath upon your cheek,
you are unaware of its presence.

I have lived so long with the elephants
      that I can no longer tell you
when they come and when they go . . ..
      Their huge bodies fill the room
and yet they move so quietly, are so

light on their wonderful feet
      that they may as well be ghosts.
When I put my face against their flanks,
      I am no more aware of them
than the lover who turns in his sleep.

At this desk I keep the trivia of memory,
      how much grain eaten, how many pounds
gained and lost. But memory is no more
      selective than the light that falls
in broken slats across the floor,

or the dust that lingers in the halls.
      How to define their absence, except
as a sadness that they leave in their wake?
      They are the stillness in an empty room,
the touch too familiar to be known.

The Touch Too Familiar

The Philosophy Professor Discusses
the Nature of the Self-Conscious Mind
(or The Invisible Bear)

"Please do not think about bears," he says,
and try as I might, here he comes, big and white,
loose jointed, lumbering over the ice flow of the page.

"And please do not consider your Social Security number
and how you are dressed at the moment," and those things,
too, come to rest beside the bear who is now sprawled

casually in the middle of the floor like a family pet,
becoming more and more familiar in all of the places
that he should not be; so I put on my coat

to cover the clothes that I am not wearing
and add my phone number to the list of trivia
that I am supposed to suppress, and try not to remember

the biologist who once explained how an invisible
object, like a polar bear, can appear white, and suddenly
I am snow-blind in Ohio. Now the bear tilts his head,

confidently, as if he knows the answer to some question,
and now he has forgotten the answer and is content
to snuzzle between the pads of one fat paw.

Already I can smell the pungency of wet fur,
can feel his cold nose in my ear, and I know for a fact
that Kant, Kierkegaard, and Sartre all owned bears,

big, fat, slumbering creatures whose paws twitched
in their sleep as they contemplated essence versus
existence among polar seals, and in my mind

I have already accepted him as a plush reality,
have already bought him a bed, checked his teeth,
paid the vet. All that is left is to name him.

In a Literary Voice

She stands in the doorway, eyebrow raised,
holding her essay at arm's length
like a subpoena. "No offense, Mrs. Essinger,
but what does this say? Why did you dot
the *C* in this word, and why did you
write *frog* all over my paper?" I sigh

and offer to translate my handwriting,
but today even I will admit that my
abbreviation for *fragment* could be *frog*,
that all of my *m's* look like *w's*
and that the *ing* lounging along the line
resembles a small lizard, tail hanging

loosely into the margin. Apostrophes fall
like shooting stars, *t's* miss their crossbows,
while *i's*, *e's* and *l's* are all interchangeable.
I confess that *trust* can look like *lust*
if you want it to, and *love, lose,*
and *leave* could all be the same.

I try to explain that words are nothing . . .
merely the tacks that hold ideas
in cognitive space. If some misunderstanding
seems to make sense, there is no loss.
A new mental geography takes over
and found logic is certainly better

than none at all. Why, even the Greek word
logos has been misread so many times
that no one knows anymore which civilization

should be in question, or who should accept
the blame. Who am I to question
the slippery logic of the literary mind?

She grimaces, rolls her eyes, shifts
the weight of her bookbag, sighs, then
reads over my shoulder, "God waits . . .
in a little red wagon"? "Yes!" I concur.
"If you want Him to, and it might also read,
'Good writing in a literary voice.'"

English 123 Discusses Virginia Woolf

Having read all the poems about starlings
and bats who fall down chimneys,
and the frantic attempts by poets

to open windows and doors, hoping
that the creature will thread some needle,
blunder into freedom, I should be prepared

for the wasp who cruises across the classroom,
raising goosebumps, causing students to shrink
and cringe, giving her safe passage

to the head of the class. She descends
from the ceiling, black and Victorian,
dragging her skirts, regal and stern,

and settles on a copy of *Roget's Thesaurus*.
I tip a coffee cup over her. She simmers
inside that little pot while students bump

around with Virginia Woolf,
stinging at the edges of *Mrs. Dalloway*
and *To the Lighthouse*, marking passages,

raising little welts in the text,
while she sizzles and mumbles to herself,
hearing voices from afar. Finally

the students close their books,
walk away, taking their voices with them,
and I carry her out into the courtyard.

I raise the cup. She pauses for a moment,
adjusts the crepe around her neck, walks
the circle where the cup has been,

and then, after checking her pockets
for stones, steps onto the invisible
staircase, and into the air . . .

David

I can't remember his last name; it won't come—
the boy who sat in the back row, frightened,
but cocky, ready to bolt if the course became
too much. David . . . Calley, Cadel, Cadence?

What was his name? It was like a chant, a song . . .
the boy who cradled a robin's egg in his pocket,
hoping to hatch it against the warmth of his skin.
The boy who derived the equation before

the questions were asked, who wrote furiously
on his exams, not because he did not know the answer,
but because he knew too many answers—
earth-wind-fire type answers.

Afraid, if he gave only one he would be
imprisoned by knowledge recognized as true
and heretic to all other forms of knowing,
and so he wrote frantically, page after page,

his hand cupped over the egg in his pocket,
his head bent over the angry page.
You want answers? I'll give you answers!
His eyes were bright with ecstasy and fear.

His hand cramped over wild sentences
that he tried desperately to punctuate
with tangled arrows, stars and dashes—
a flood of sentences, a torrent of ideas,

then me looking, looking for the right word,
clue or sign that would let me say,
"Yes, yes, you've passed my course,"
while he read over my shoulder, disappointed,

thrilled, amazed that I found his work
acceptable, and then rejecting the approval
he crushed the paper in one hand and cried,
"How can you know? How can you possibly know?"

Art History 121

"Reality is a slippery subject," the professor says,
as he walks across the darkened stage, intersecting
the dusty beams of twin projectors. Now the victim,

the man about to be executed in Goya's *The Third
of August*, is pictured on the teacher's shirt as he
uses the shadow of his own outstretched hand

to show how the perspective is all wrong . . . or just
right, depending on how you look at it. If the man
would just stand up, he could overwhelm the militia

who fill the right foreground of the painting, but they
will not turn toward us, nor will the priest who bows
his head to bless the dead. When the instructor looks

away, we pass whispers and promises up the darkened
aisle, while he fumbles for a slide from another era.
The projector clicks and whines, the room brightens,

and now the militia aim their rifles across the stage
at the *Odalisque,* whose face floats above the teacher's head,
while his hand hovers along the curve of her thigh

and we, less curious about art than anatomy, would count
the elongated vertebrae in her spine, if he would just hold
still for a moment, would let the light fall naturally

into our new reality. But now he stands like a time traveler,
before a woods, circa 1850, and an ox cart fords a stream
just ahead of a thunderstorm, and the rainbow is almost

beyond the reach of his index finger, which sweeps
the screen like the hand of an angel . . . and then with a flick
of his thumb we careen into the industrial era and Turner's

"tinted steam" reddens our faces, and we forget the air
conditioned chill of the room where we crouch, arms around
our knees, jackets thrown like shawls over bare limbs.

Fourth Position, Grande Jeté

The room is so small and poorly lit that only a few
can get close enough to lean on the locked case,
so I see her first as a shadow on the museum wall.

She looks like a seamstress with her head
bent against the light, intent on some needlework
that folds into the shadows of those who pass by,

or perhaps a mother motioning with curled
fingers for a child to come a bit closer, to sit
for a moment, please, beside her and try to be still.

But, from this angle, she appears to be walking
through crowded streets, head raised, arms circling
a large bundle, a basket, perhaps, of laundry or linen.

And she walks with the grace of one who knows
that she is being watched, but doesn't care,
for this moment belongs to her, not to the artist.

So when I finally meet her in the museum case,
she already seems oddly familiar, as I bend
to examine this bronze in fourth position,

grand jeté, and now the sculpture itself
seems almost an offense, so crudely done,
the clay patchy and rough, with Degas's fingerprints

in bronze and all of the technique showing through.
This is not the woman I met in the shadows,
moving from pose to pose. Now she has been stilled

forever in this position, impossible to hold.
And I want to ask her, how did this happen?
Why these pinches, these smudges along your thigh?

Who tilted your head, raised your cheekbones
with his thumbs, then left you here, for the sake of art,
a diary of all of the ways that he has touched you?

Nude On A Couch

"Where did she get those boots?" the boy asks,
and the guide, positioned rather awkwardly
with a group of third graders beside Caillebotte's
reclining nude, has to look twice to be sure
that there are indeed boots in the painting,
one upright, the other leaning slightly
beside the embroidered sofa where the young
woman is enjoying her own nakedness.

The sofa is a wide ottoman, banded
with braid and cording, the pillows so large
and firm that the woman's form barely depresses
the cushions, a flaw perhaps in the artist's
technique, if the sofa were not so exquisite,
her skin so perfectly soft and pale.

She has placed a cushion to pillow her head
and now reclines, while her left arm shades
her eyes and her right hand fondles the nipple
of her left breast. Her clothes seem recently
discarded, and indeed, her skirt and undergarments
can be seen heaped upon the cushions, a detail
that the classicist would find too intimate,
too offensive. And yet,

one can almost feel the pinch of the shirtwaist,
can follow the pale softness of belly and thigh,
past the leg resting against the back of the sofa
to the feet, and the guide is surprised
that it took a child's question to remind him,
for it is her feet that intrigue him,

the pink heels, the arch enhanced by shadow
and the toes turned up in this moment
of pleasure . . . but the boots,

of course, why hadn't he noticed before?
The boots explain this woman lost
in a moment of erotic solitude, her body
slender but unremarkable, slack and tender,
surrounded by everyday clothing, the pinch
of the streets, the confines of expectations,
and the boots that say, Yes, yes, you might meet
her in a shop; you might meet her anywhere.

In These Paintings By David . . .

In these paintings by David, one is forever pushed
and pulled. See Marat asleep (no, murdered!)
in his bath. The serenity of his face, the circle
of his arms, the pen still dripping in one hand,
make death seem like a gentle settling into place.

Only the tilt of his head, a certain slackness
along the jaw, and the wound, a crimson slit,
that skirts the shadow of his chest, betray
the death . . . and, of course, the pearl-handled knife,
almost invisible in the darkened foreground.

Now look at Socrates on his deathbed, right arm raised
above his head as a stern finger chides his guests,
warns them that this is not the moment to weaken
and turn away, even though the man who extends the cup
of hemlock hides his face, his very body refusing

to comply. Or is Socrates' finger pointing heavenward
through the dusty light and the distant archway
that fills the background of the painting?
And who are these people who are unafraid to watch,
the eager faces that fill the foreground on the right?

Should we look or turn away? Socrates with his graying
head and neoclassical body draped in white compels
us to watch. Marat's outstretched arms invite us
into the intimacy of the moment. Only later,
do we see death sitting at the end of the bed,

another version of Socrates, his body slack with age,
his face saddened, his head bent in reflection.
Only later do we see the water tinged with Marat's
blood, the glint of the knife, the length of
the dark blade, the courage and the tenderness.

Watercolor

Peter Spier, your *Noah's Ark* is not a pretty story.
"An illustrator's dream," you said, "the animals,
the storm, the rainbow at the end."
The truth you didn't tell hangs
in another room where Noah plugs his ears
against the screams of the dying,
and elephants stand knee-deep in rain
with smaller creatures on their backs.

You painted them all without guilt—
there is only wonder in their eyes
and the innocence of fear,
for in fear all things become innocent
and rainbows are hard won.

So I pack my ark against the flood,
against fear, and innocence, and madness.
Inside I have only singular things,
nothing that comes in pairs:
      some fairy tales
      my sons
      an arrowhead
      a chickadee, found dead,
and a cardinal that pecks at my door
demanding his little bit of forever.
So I open the door and let him in,
but around us there is only fear,
innocence, and the color of water.

A Response to Critics

Early morning, late in September, and the day so dark
it feels like night. The porch light illuminates
the foreground, and in a moment the begonias will become
famous, the focal point in some artist's painterly display.

A few leaves, artfully placed, a potted fern, and the painting
acquires its depth. A rough table tries to slip away into
the shadows, but the artist has caught it. Two dry strokes
and the background is fixed between night and day.

Now, step over the sill and into this still life by Renoir.
The air is damp against our cheeks, the night as cool
as a museum hall. Beyond this frame there are art historians
and the bump and pull of dark ideas, thoughts that must

be translated into the grammar of the discipline,
but here the leaves are still flat against the walk,
and although the table tilts oddly, the space is narrow,
the canvas rough, everything remains safely two dimensional.

But far away tail lights smear their phosphorescent glow
inside another frame, and someone comes to take us away.
He gets out a knife and cuts away the canvas, lifts us
into a car, and now there is a new artist in charge,

a Chagal perhaps, or maybe a Degas. The light is still
bright, of course, everything up close and intimate,
the upholstery imitating the feel of the canvas,
but now we are on a ramp, approaching the freeway

and some Warhol has picked up his brush and is throwing
paint onto the windshield—slick and glossy and alive—
and the night is a moving canvas as kind and minimal
as black vinyl, and we have all come along for the ride.

On The Beach

As a liberal-arts major all of my life,
I take great comfort in knowing
that the astronauts are out there,
patching the Hubble telescope
with 100-mph duct tape and string.

For that matter, I want to meet
the man who first slid a human heart
into a Playmate Cooler and stepped
onto a commercial flight. Did he confess
to the attendant or did she assume
bologna and cheese and a six pack?

Is it really such a leap from archaeology
to leftovers? If Tupperware can preserve
last week's pickled beets, why not
a prehistoric brain? Resourcefulness
is overrated . . .Why, even I might have
thought of Superglue, when Freddie
the Pelican flew home with a broken bill.

And if Max the gorilla at the Toledo zoo
is having trouble reproducing his kind,
a little porno flick from the Congo
might do him good. If his mate,
hand raised in Philadelphia,
has become so civilized that she doesn't
know which end is up, put the baby
in Pampers and give her a break.
Everyone has shortcomings.

Even math majors forget
to balance checkbooks and who knows
if the scientists are right?
Despite their smug superiority,

is anyone really going to question
data gathered from the outer
reaches of the solar system?

It's easy to be critical I suppose
when one has chosen a safe profession.
I've never neglected to thaw out
someone's embryo, or mistyped blood,
or accused someone of a crime
because I misread the DNA scan.
No lives hang in the balance
if I misquote Yeats or forget
who wrote *The Ring and the Book.*

But at the end, when the software
fails and the radiation is rising,
I think that even an English major
will be resourceful enough to loop
the string of the window sash to the neck
of the Coke bottle, balanced
to tap out some erratic Morse Code
to a world half annihilated
by the wonders of modern science.

The Intimacy of Strangers

The Intimacy of Strangers

At 20,000 feet suede brushes
against tweed . . . and we sit closer
than lovers, knee to knee,
while behind us the Junior Executive
discusses stocks and bonds
and explains that "two hundred
from the home office will have to go,"
and the coed sitting next to him
seems to be falling for it,
while we rise through the gray sleet
of Chicago, above two-car garages
and ranch-style homes with swimming pools.

The gray at your temple fades
into dusky curls that fall
too close to your collar, a bit
frayed, a little too snug
for comfort. I tug at the suede
that covers too little, and now
too much, of one knee and wonder
who lies down with you at night,
while the pretty coed swears
she could never "do anything
quite as wonderful as all that,"
and we continue to discuss
Chicago, children, colleagues . . .

But at 30,000 feet everything is make-
believe, cotton candy and spun glass
with clouds that almost touch
and when the young steward steps
into the aisle, to whisper into
another attendant's ear, he steadies
her with hands that slide
from her shoulders down to her hips,
while she deftly pours a ginger
ale and lifts her cheek, so
the whisper can become a kiss.

"Are You My Angel?"

Allen Ginsberg
"A Supermarket In California"

I have never seen Walt Whitman "poking
among the meats," but I saw Gorbachev
yesterday at the grocery store
palming heads of lettuce. Raisa stood
beside him, still wearing her winter
furs, despite an early spring.

And once I saw Einstein weighing
coffee beans at Anderson's on Senior
Citizen Discount Day, and Solzhenitsyn
at Quality Farm and Fleet, testing
the nuts and bolts, his great sad face
intent on some tiny mechanism.

I've recognized Billie Jean King
and Gloria Steinem often enough
to make me wonder if they are stalkers.
And it's true, I talk to Kurt Vonnegut
at the local library. I try to stand
beside him, when the librarian
scratches his card across the register,
hoping to catch a few titles.

What is Kurt reading nowadays?
Forest Hunter? Kundera? *Everything
You Need To Know About Home Repair*?
He strokes his mustache, shrugs

his shoulders and turns his palms out,
as if to say, The deck is rotting,
the plumbing leaks . . . "poo-tee-weet."

When I try to explain to my husband,
he rolls his eyes and snaps the paper
off the cheese with measured impatience.
"You need a rest," he says, "Take a walk";
so I fold my hands like Emily
and try to look distant and chaste.

I won't tell him that I saw our neighbor,
Maggie Keller, on the Troy-Urbana Road.
I smiled and waved and she smiled back.
She has been dead for over a year now,
but I would know her gray-blonde curls
anywhere, and those long slim fingers
draped over the steering wheel.

For Six Friends

When I come back to haunt you,
I promise it will be a gentle haunting . . .
no bloody crosses on the wall to frighten
you into the arms of religion, no unearthly

moans or thunder to keep you awake.
No need to carry talismans in your pockets.
I won't have you trembling before cellar
doors, or avoiding moonlit nights.

But when November comes, to pick the lock
between the living and the dead, notice
please, the door that whinnies on its hinge,
the book that turns its own pages,

the moth that hovers beside your chin.
Talk to me when the cat stares at some
nothingness beyond, when daylight fades
and leaves move against the wind.

And when women gather beside the fire,
to weave the truths and lies that make
them friends, set the table with Haviland
and old silver, and pull up an extra chair.

You Are Right

In your super-logical
analytical,
bumbling way,
with halting speech
and much digression,
you explain that male
mathematicians are rarely
verbal . . .

>   "oh by the way,
>   did I mention that this theory
>   is largely unproven, but
>   nevertheless, quite probable?"

because of a prenatal
super-dose of testosterone
to the left side of the brain
which suppresses the right
side of the brain
where you are currently
trying to express
your lack of verbal agility

while at the same time
peeling an orange,
stroking your mustache,
pulling your ear,
and making little
finger-steeples.

And I am about to conclude
that you are right.

The Mathematician, Counting

One cannot help loving a mathematician.
Such guts, such pizzaz!
Plump Copernicus, full of round theories;
Euclid, pondering his postulates
and counting, always counting
toward a finite infinity.

All the while, the heart's
little time bomb is busy,
adding and subtracting.
I have seen both the sun
and the moon in the morning sky.
What does this prove?
Some superstition?
Some old astronomer's tale?
No, no . . . only proof of our spinning—
the geometry of the universe.

It is August.
The meadows are afloat
with Queen Anne's Lace,
each a starry galaxy.
We are an equation devoted to itself,
a myriad of seeds, lives, stars,
bursting their pods,
each capable, countable,
inchoate,
an endless census,
a mathematical fecundity
in which decades are the norm.
And each is devoted to the count,
always the count, the counting
theory holds, even if infinity should fail.

Morning News

Three Stories That Deserve Better Telling

"Sorry, sorry, too tired to write
        I know this story deserves better telling.
It's hard to live my life and write about it too."
        E-mail from L.A.

I

Daybreak begins in some small town east
of here where the birds rise earlier
and leaves have lain all night, waiting
for this first poor light, tipped
like little satellite dishes eager
for any bit of late-breaking news.
I know this story deserves better telling,
but by the time our doves begin to stir
making their daily schlep from the feeder
to the sill, the sun is old news.
No notes on the bedside table, no clues.
Sorry, sorry, too tired to write.

II

I know this story is hard to tell.
The morning news reports a drive-by
shooting and an old murder, discovered
overnight, a woman's remains encased
in concrete on the seventh floor,
of the *Daily News*, Fourth and Ludlow.
Weary reporters interview themselves . . . "Sorry,
sorry . . . how long did you know the suspect?
Did you ever see him in the building

after hours, did you ever meet his wife?"
Is it hard to live your life and write it too?
I know this story; it deserves better telling.

III

"Sorry, sorry, too tired to write,"
E-mail messages from both coasts
recount your midnight trek from New Jersey
to L.A., time lost in the East never reclaimed,
missed flights, new connections, reservations
gone to travelers whose flights come in on time,
and your friend throttles the night clerk
and demands this tiny basement room reserved
for others, and only this late night/early morning
note to explain, "Sorry, sorry . . . too tired . . .
it's hard to live the story and tell it too."

From the Top of the Hill

Here, on the curb, at dusk, two boys
on bikes race to cross five lanes of a city street,
while a car at the bottom of a short, steep hill
snags gears and slides through the light. Headlights
flash, wheels sparkle, and the first—older, taller—
pedals quickly to safety, but the second
lags behind, caught in the blur
between night and day.

I step into the street,
mouth open, unable to speak, too many words
for what needs to be said, caught
in my throat, and I remember
there is always one left to tell
and how naive I am to think
this will always be me or one of mine,
and I remember my own sons, sliding
out of my life, as I try to speak.

In the streetlight
I see the boy's bare back, the delicate
weave of bone and muscle not yet man,
feel my hand run down his spine,
though he is still beyond reach.
The car tops the hill, his shoulders buck,
he stands on the brakes, throws the wheel
and drops, barefoot, to straddle
the center line, while the car slides by
in gray, all windows and doors,

and I am still here
beside the curb, though the boys
have long since called to one another
and gone on, but thoughts come tangled,
bulky and slow, like the bike
that was much too large, blue, I think,
and as he pedaled his arms rose about his face
like a swimmer's in deep water, and his chin
dipped, like this, between the silver bars.

Running

Three miles out on a country road
you no longer look like my son.
Your back is so lean,
your legs so strong. You pump
some energy up from the blacktop,
your hair swinging a small arc
across your back, your arms rocking.

At the crossroads you turn toward home
the neighbor's chocolate Lab
panting at your feet. His mission
is simple—"follow any boy."
At home your dog sleeps
in the shade of the porch.
She is plump, but loyal.
She rushes to meet you,
sprints the last thirty yards
then pants for praise.

Too tired to move
you fluff her up with words,
"You wuss, you big fat wuss!"
while the Lab falls in the grass,
tongue wide as a platter.
He seems confused.
How could this have happened?
Wrong house, wrong boy.
I bring him a drink,
finger his ears, and promise
him a ride home in the car.

Around us is the stillness of evening,
corn and mint, and in the pond
a blue heron steps so lightly
he leaves no ripple—
only the memory of motion.
For a moment we are timeless,
you and me and the trusting dogs.
There is only this road, this night
and you are my son forever.

Patching the Sky

Up on the roof you are patching the sky
with scraps of scratchy black.
But here, beneath the barn's high dome
it may as well be night—sweet hay
beneath my feet and overhead a thousand
stars where chips of light slip through
the shingled cracks.

Your pockets are full of tacks—stars
in a carpenter's apron. I hear your hammer
like sharp, fast, rain, winking out
the stars one by one, and through the cracks
can almost see the silver circle
as it pivots in your hand, righting
itself for the next blow.

Thunder scrapes along the eaves as you
drag your ladder to the next horizon.
Bent and broken nails squeak and cry
as you hunt them down, yank at their roots,
and nail the darkness back into place.

Finally, the dome is dark;
the patter of old shoes is rain,
muffling the approach of day.
The heavy door slides by—you stand alone
with light clinging to your trousers
and dawn settling about your feet.

Letter to Jerry

Do you remember the mouse we found
under a loose brick, beside your back door?
Flattened, frozen dry . . . stepped on,
God knows how many times.
You held him up by his tail,
thin and flat as a maple leaf . . .
a delicate horror.
As you tossed him into a pile of leaves
you muttered an awkward blessing.
"Beware what you seek, for you shall find."

Did you believe in immortality—
that ultimate of thrifts?
I doubt it.

Somewhere I have a picture of you
carrying buckets of water to the barn
so you can thaw the pump and water your sheep.
The steam has frozen on your clothes;
your face is red with cold.
We were always too cautious
with one another.
Knowing perhaps, if we could give or take
twenty years, what might have been.

You used to call me Katie.
I don't know why;
it is not my name.

I dragged stories out of you
the way one removes the bottom book
from a tall stack . . . quickly,
hoping the entire pile will
slip down a notch and not
topple from the jolt . . .
     the oldest, the drunkest,
     the sexiest (The worst:

your friend who wears a hood
to hide his scars from Auschwitz).
You were casual, yet precise in the telling,
the way one measures salt into the palm
of the hand.

At night we went out to watch
the meteor showers. Lord, but it was cold.
You never wanted to come, saying
"Some things are not meant to be seen,
and I'm too old to be star struck."
But I would insist, and you would come
grudgingly, muttering under your breath,
"May the Lord protect us from his grace."
We sat with our backs together,
teepee style,
each watching and calling out.
We saw our own, but never each other's.

There is a trick to seeing stars—
the eye's fovea tires so quickly
one must learn to look askance,
or the stars fade
even as you gaze.

On the night that you died
I looked for you everywhere—
the greenhouse, the creek, the mill,
and finally in town.
It was a strange evening, late in August,
about the time those midnight-blue
butterflies begin to fly.
A warmth remained, long past sunset,
like the warmth that remains
in a chair when the guest is gone.
In town, sprinklers were spidering
across the park; children were catching fireflies.
But something had changed.
I could see it in faces

as people hurried up their walks,
grateful for the door
they could pull behind them.

I wish you were here to advise me on my garden.
It has grown completely out of hand.
Gophers have made a mess of the corn.
The zucchini are hard and heavy.
They swell at night when they
think I'm not looking.
I thunk them with my thumb.
It is going to frost soon:
  You can see it in the air—
  a certain odd transparency,
  much like frozen fruit.

The nights are perfect for star gazing,
and so, here I am again,
looking for shooting stars . . .
that momentary flash that transfixes.
Something compels me to watch them die.
I don't really want to look,
but when I cover my eyes,
it is black, black as a planetarium,
and I am afraid of what I do not see.

Now more than ever, I am in need of your blessing:
"Dearest Katie, may the Lord protect you from his grace."

I Don't Remember Taking This Picture

even though it is my shadow which falls
    across the step, but I like
        the way my father is sitting,
            knees together, feet apart.

He is making a lap for my mother's
    black cat who is young in the picture,
        but who has since been buried
            in the little pet cemetery

to the left, out of the picture,
    under the trees where sweet peas and
        peonies bloom among the small mounds,
            and despite his straw hat and boots,

my father's pose is almost feminine.
    He is stroking the cat who is happy
        for the attention, while my mother stands
            beside him holding a glass of wine.

She is wearing her favorite cotton blouse,
    which has since become a garden shirt.
        She is looking into the camera,
            but Father is lowering his head

to see if the cat is enjoying this moment
    on the step. I don't remember when the picture
        replaced the memory, or if the memory ever
            existed at all, or merely recreated itself

from the photo, the way a negative can
    recreate its positive, the way light distilled
        from an instant can be brought back
            into the present, but now I can no longer

remember the cat except as he appears in the photo,
    as he flattens himself beneath my father's
        hand so the fingers can reach further
            into the pleasure of the moment.

For My Brother,
Reading Over My Shoulder

When you stand like this, one arm braced
against the table, head bent against the light,
shading the page, you take the words away,
suck the meanings out until they dissolve
into the familiar, like memories of childhood.
Letters cling to the page like weathered husks,
like the locust shells we used to gather
in Kansas, piling them into pails and wagons
as if absence could become its own harvest.

We plucked them from the maples where they sat
like little trolley cars, abandoned at some station,
and we studied their emptiness, the slit
between the shoulders where the escape was made,
leaving behind the crisp tobacco case,
perfectly tucked, molded around a presence
we could only imagine in the bubbled eyes,
the pleated legs, the intricate mouth
and claw that still could frighten—

all evidence that we, too, could be transformed,
could get out safely with only words left
to explain how the maples shaded our horizons,
how the oaks grew so huge that they tilted
the sidewalks, and childhood disappeared,
dissolved so abruptly into the present,
that now there is only this memory and you,
reading in this ambered light, to remind me
that once we stood there, once we were young.

Lions

I

Sometimes at night we thought them thunder,
        their voices echoing across the river,
first the dull rumble, like gravel in a chute,
        then the huge mouthy roar that gathers
around you like a summer night, flush and warm
        against your cheek, and then we remembered
that there were lions in the dark, their voices
        amplified by distance and the cages
that kept them in their places, and we knew
        that we were young, and vulnerable.

II

Mr. Linke, blinded by a hunting accident,
        years ago, knew us each by the sound
of our step on his walk. I never spoke to him
        unless he spoke first, and only once
did he stop me on the sidewalk with his cane,
        ask my name, ask if my dogs were barking
across the street, ask if I ever heard lions
        in the dark, and then I knew that he was lost
on a familiar street and it was night
        and someone would have to see him home.

III

Years later, in a summer classroom in another
        state, I am filling a blue book, turning
the pages against the clock, writing everything
        I know about Milton and *Paradise Lost,*
while night noises tick against the window
        and upstairs someone is shoving boxes
across a wooden floor, a sound that gathers
        then retreats, like gravel in a chute
or the echo of thunder, pacing itself
        against time and distance, and once again
there is a blind man at my elbow asking,
        "Do you ever hear lions in the dark?"

Biography

I frame these moments in words, as if
they were photographs that could be placed
in your hand upon your return, and yet
in your absence, they do not seem real . . .
the grass that shimmers, the trees that filter
the evening light, the dog who comes wading
through the weeds, her legs wet with dew.

See how the window divides the view
as if it were on an easel, the hummingbird
perfectly placed between drawn panels,
the willow creating its own diagonal
across the canvas. It is all beautiful,
but no more real than canned peaches on the shelf
that press their faces against the glass.

How the light loves those bruised cheeks,
the tender hollow where the seed once slept.
Tonight the peach trees drop their
fruit like velvet buttons in the grass,
and I have been reading Virginia Woolf,
trying to understand the nature of loss and its
relationship to biography, since everyone,

of course, is writing his own,
and the story says, Yes . . .this is important,
even these little things belong in the story.
So I gather the little peaches . . .the small,
the unborn . . .and pocket them for the present,
while up above the others swell and ripen,
pacing themselves against your return.

Not to Reply

September, birds and shadows.
The sky has become an Escher print
where everything is suspended
between what it is

and what it is becoming.
In the next room you are discussing
a book I have never read.
I do not like

the sound of your voice.
I step out hoping not to see
the bird that stumbled against
the glass. It is dull on top,

but underneath a peachy cream.
It struggles with wings thrown back,
mouth open, tiny claws
hooking at the air.

It makes all of the moves
that ought to set a bird upright,
while others stand about,
curious at such distress.

We offer no advice. Winter is coming.
Small things are learning how to die.
You call from the door—I practice
reasons not to reply.

Growing Accustomed to Green

Growing Accustomed to Green

Once your eyes grow accustomed to green
    the surprise is not
        that you did not see him

but that you did not see him before
    for, in truth, he looks
        nothing like a tomato leaf.

His hooded head and rearing neck
    resemble a sea-horse.
        His rippling body fades

into a froth of herring bone green
    and then tapers to a sudden
        sharpness like a thorn.

In fact, only his feet, clamped
    about this stem, resemble
        the joining of leaves.

Still, he continues this deception—
    it is the only guile he knows
        and now that you have grown familiar

now that green is no longer
    an oddity, but the one charm
        that is always given,

when you look away, into
    the splash of field and meadow
        doesn't everything else appear

    changed, wild and strange?

Ladders

for my father

Always I am standing
at the foot of the ladder
      where everything is passed down.

Today it is cherries
pulled from that green attic
      that you planted so long ago.

I empty the battered bucket
and hand it up again . . . always this
      rising up, this bringing down.

There are too many; we can eat no more,
and I have stood so long
      with my arms stretched over my head

that when I bring them down
it is like a little death.
      Now it is dark; doors are closing.

I hear the ladder creak
beneath your weight, sigh
      as you turn away. But look,

see how the little seckle pear throws
her children in the air, feet first.
      When she tires, we lift them down.

Tomorrow there will be apples and pears,
bushels to fill . . . always
      this rising up, this bringing down.

Alice Reads to the Daffodils

Reflected in the silver vase
the newspaper diminishes
like the prow of a boat
headed for dark water.
She reads aloud,
pausing occasionally to study
the daffodils that tip
their heads attentively.
The headlines are worrisome
for those who come in ruffles.
Violence blooms on every street
corner . . . silent, beautiful,
the flowers
huddle like young men
with knives in their pockets.
What do they know about April,
here, where the light is
so unpredictable
and someone returns them
to the icebox every evening?
Still, there is the urgency
of spring, the rustle
of moonlight on city streets,
the silver blade in hand.
Soon, the hollow stem,
the paper sheath,
the green knotted joint,
then the flash of bloom,
so quick
it is almost bloodless.

Blue Lakes and Scarlet Runners

Here, at the blossom end
    of the universe where
everything lives and dies,
      I set some clock to ticking,

swing some pendulum into motion.
    The seeds float in my hand
oblivious to earthly time,
      but behind me lies an uneven

basted line, stitches meant
    to burrow in, take hold,
until something moist
      tethers them to this

dark moment, Blue Lakes and
    Scarlet Runners, and at the end
of the row, a crescent
      moon, pale and low.

I push them in with my thumb,
    feel the earth fold in around
and touch the puckered scar
      where the umbilical lets go.

Talking to Flowers

(200 miles with a vase of peonies on my lap)

First we spoke about fragrance—
how the wind paints the air
with sweetness and complexity,
inhaling, exhaling . . .

Then we discussed the coolness
that comes up from the earth
and lodges in the blossom opening
like a mouth—satiny wet,
smooth as the inside of the cheek.

Then we spoke of the urgency
of the sun which yanks the stem
upward and forces the leaves
to dislodge the blossom with seeds
that confine and condense . . . everything
planned out, everything spoken for
even before it has begun.

And then we spoke about silence
and the fragile gestures made by flowers
and the single word spoken
by each blossom, mouth to mouth.

Amniotic

Two rainy days and one warm night
and suddenly the corn becomes
a standing army, a regiment
of green, soldiering its way
across the Midwest, closing in
on country lanes. We ricochet
through green canyons, skid
to unexpected stops, peer around
corners that did not exist a month ago.

And once again you explain how
the corn tassels and the pollen
drifts down to the salty silk
and impregnates the ear, each
sticky thread inventing
a single kernel, and once again
I resist knowing, despite
innumerable lessons—an ocean of green.
Still I want my bit of ignorance,

the amniotic mystery of corn,
and as I brush the silk
from sticky fingers, the sweet fibers
condense everything intuitive
into this fragrant bundle,
so we can arrive, once again,
every summer, at this place
so familiar we forget
that it exists.

Green Will

I'm teaching a piece of cucumber vine
to climb the garden fence. Every morning
I wrap the sticky tendrils around my thumb
and place the little hands upon the wire.
They hang like toddlers at a gate,

but a few are beginning to understand.
Whipped by the sun, they are forming
green fists, laying down fingers one by one,
hauling themselves upward, like little boys
doing chin-ups—more will than might.

I want this vine to go *over* the fence,
not through it, so every night I go out
and make corrections, poking stray elbows
into place and tying up delinquent strands.

But wayward stalks are getting out of hand.
They are climbing with a green, muscular hunger,
bracing themselves for a mighty upward heave.
Soon they will have a stranglehold, a murderous
grip on everything within their reach.

Soon there will be only this vine
with its green will and bitter seeds.

Double-Winged Achenes

I

Two weeks after the swallows appear
the maples drop their wings.
They twirl downward in death-
defying leaps, casualties
from the highest ledge. They cling

to our hair, tumble down shirt
sleeves, find the odd resting place
in pocket and fold, only to be found
later, like the lost ticket from
some purchase made long ago.

But unlike the plowman in Brueghel's
Icarus, some of us do look up.
We know the feel of makeshift
wings, see the flutter and fall,
hear the rustle of despair.

II

I saw a photo once of women,
children, jumping into firemen's
nets. The camera followed them
one by one, catching each for
a moment in that flickering eye.

They fell like angels with their skirts
ruffled about them, wings on fire,
while on the ground the firemen
braced themselves on the wet pavement,
arms and legs bent to accept

the coming weight, eyes fixed
on a single form, unaware of those
who had fallen about them, unaware
of the camera, which has already
caught each of us in midflight.

Today the Starlings Are Listening to Brahms . . .

a sonata in E flat minor.
Soon they will hear Chopin and Vivaldi,
courtesy of NPR and a radio
I have wedged into the top notch
of the cherry tree to distract them
from fruit still too tart for my taste.

Yesterday they heard a lecture on ecology—
the importance of the Hubble telescope
and its impact on third world countries.
They thought about these things
seriously all afternoon, sneaking only
occasional glances at the cherry tree.

Tomorrow they will hear the poets:
Frost and Stevens, Eliot and Pound,
and a few excerpts from Virginia Woolf.
They have forgotten about the cherries
that ripen below, and the sweet seeds
that rolled in their beaks like pebbles.

But I miss the sound of their voices,
those rough vowels that startle
the sparrows and rattle the morning air.
Tonight they pace the lawn and look at me
as if they would like to speak, as if
they would like to explain about the cherries,

how sweet they are on bird tongues,
how stolen fruit has always been theirs
for the taking, no crime in taking
that which is freely given. But their mouths
open and won't close, and they turn away,
with words still caught in their throats.

As I Try to Explain, No Words Come Out

*Experiments . . . show that no pigment can be found in blue jay
feathers. Scientists . . . assume that the blue in the blue jay comes
from light scattering, a process of refraction and retransmission
of light by transparent objects.*

Science News, Nov. 1, 1986

On PBS, I learn
that color is to light
what pitch is to sound,
so today the blackbird
on this branch,
absorbing all visible light,

whistles one low note after another,
    and the maples
that once absorbed everything
    but green,
now bounce back noisy
    reds and yellows,
and the roses suck in
    so much light
they hum fluorescent,

but the blue jay must be invisible,
    for blue is not blue,
but the absence of blue,
    refraction versus reflection,
light scattered by transparent objects.

So tonight as he perches on this wet rail,
perfectly balanced between light and song,
    his beak opens and closes,
    but no song is seen
    no light heard.

Drought

I found him first in the orphan's corner,
    that sheltered nook beside the front door
where every lost thing eventually reappears.
    I carried him to the porch, slid him in
under the evergreens where a brown lump,
    if he's cautious, may go unnoticed all summer.

But, sometimes I hear him late at night—
    a rustle in the leaves, then the dry scrabble
of toad toes as he climbs the steps,
    then belly flops into the water bowl,
where I will find him in the morning, dozing,
    riding the surface tension of the water,

chin propped against the slick bowl where
    even his sticky toes cannot obtain a grip.
A tiny bubble forms at the tip of his chin
    as he floats, unaware of blue jays and squirrels
and slobbering dogs who claim the same rights
    by day. He trusts in divine intervention.

I dump him rudely into the leaves where,
    camouflaged by ivy and geraniums, he examines
me for a moment. I am the most dependable
    mystery in his life. He is slouched and comical,
low-slung, a leathery bag that folds in upon itself,
    no bigger than a handful of marbles.

He has all of the beauty of a clod of dirt,
    except for the creamy kidded leather
at his chin and throat where his pulse taps

out some lucky rhythm. I want to explain
that I do not believe in the hand of fate,
    or faith, or even in luck itself,

but his jetted eye follows me as I clean
    the bowl, wipe the sides, and refill
this little reservoir in the middle
    of a Midwest drought, and his thin lips
tuck so smoothly into the corners
    of his cheeks that I think he smiles.

Phases of the Moon

cold night, kitchen light,
winter lake, wafer shape,
door knob, miner's light

nectarine, nursery rhyme,
egg yolk, cantaloupe,
baby's sock, lemon drop

chipped plate, crescent roll,
lily's fold, banana bowl,
silver spoon, slice of pie

goblet rim, firefly,
owl's wing, sleepy eye,
cold light, kitchen night.

Moon Garden

The moon is out.
The baby is asleep.
Everything about his face
      is crescent shaped.
He sleeps with his hands
      in the air, afloat.
His thoughts are as weightless
      as the color of blue
      in water.

Last night we named every color
in the garden: red, orange, yellow, green.

He laughed and laughed . . .
he thought I had invented them.

It was a game . . .
I was the name giver,

and I laughed too . . .
seeing how he had invented me.

His smile, that smooth buckle, bound us.
moon-garden; baby-me.

Equinox

First you find a solid, level surface.
Concrete is good. Then, balancing the egg
between thumb and forefinger, you coax
it into an upright position, settling
the yolk into the curve of the shell,
coddling the embryo until it drops

like the moon into the bend of the horizon.
And you hold so still that the cat molds
himself between your legs and the baby,
asleep along the curve of arm, melds
into your flesh until you can no longer
tell where baby ends and breast begins.

For a breathless moment the egg stands,
and everything perilous seems possible,
until the moon drops, the shell breaks,
and the cat cries out, once again, afraid.

Eclipse

In Jamaica,
Columbus bargained with the Indians,
trading moonlight for rice and beans,
and they, thinking him a god,
thanked him for his compassion.

Tonight,
we sit with fruit and cheese
half eaten in our laps
and watch the earth pare away
the last slice of summer moon.

The goddess
Diana has left for the hunt, shooting
moonbeams from her crescent bow.
We have no hope of her return,
and having killed all local deities

with disbelief,
we sit alone in the dark, wondering
what is left to bargain with
and if any god loves us enough
to make the light return.

Coincidence

coming as it does
coincidentally, can make us
believe in almost anything . . .

religion, magic, stars, Magi,
all post hoc, of course,
random results, and yet,

empirical, observable.
and if we believed
the sun circled the earth

every 24 hours
was it really
such bad science?

Occasionally
a crow paces
his way across the lawn
with such purpose

we know
he is on a mission
from someplace unknown,

or the pear tree blossoms
with such fragility
that we choose on the spot

to believe
in almost anything
post magic, post science.

And if
with failing sight
you call me to the window
to say, look . . .

look at the hawk;
see how he hangs
on that limb

and I know
it is not a hawk,
but a common bird

that rests here everyday,
is it really any less
hawklike?

Two Apples

One evening
when the air was still

two apples blossomed
so close to one another

that an uncontrolled
green doubling

caused them to merge
one into the other.

All summer we guarded
this orchard oddity,

thinking ourselves twice-blessed,
until late in August

we picked the twins
and slid the knife

along the welt
that belonged to both

and bit
into a galaxy of seeds,

and there among the rings
and swirls

we could see how
desperately

they had tried
to grow apart.

Fences

Even as he sank the last post
he remembered fences
broken,

the ones that sagged
as if they had been ridden
too long

or the ones that simply dropped
crushed
by the weight of the sky

while others were raised up
dispossessed
by the ground itself

or were engulfed
by tangled green complexities
knottings beyond all untangling

or swallowed whole
by trees
that lay down next to them,

and remembering
he twisted
the wire quite tight.

Clearing the Garden

The sunflowers are the first to come down.
    Grand, yet somehow grotesque, they buckle
and pitch forward, scattering seeds like currency.
    All summer the stalks strained to keep
the heavy heads aloft, while the seeds
      longed daily for the ground.

Spiders spread their webs among the corn.
    What can they find here, late in October?
Flies are as scarce as money on the wind.
    The squash have collapsed, leaves blackened.
Only the kale remains green, and it is an oddity.
    We dig potatoes, find arrowheads among the onions.

A toad, drowsing in a pile of leaves, is stilled
    by the cold. He is waiting, like the others—
still as a stone, cool as a penny, a chip of remembrance.
    When I pick him up to set him aside, I feel
his pulse in my palm, and his skin seems to sag
    with a loose, almost genital softness.

Dry Creek Bed

remembering the motion of water
   the rocks rise up
      shoulder the morning sun
         tumble against one another

ride the empty current downstream
   past the roots of sycamore,
      under the rusting bridge
         among clotted vines

we step from stone to stone
   the memory of roughened water
      becomes the motion
         of ankles, hips, thighs

we name things no longer
   here: the sound of water
      the flitting minnows, the snake
         that slept beneath this stone

here among this polished absence
   I lift a palm shaped stone
      hold it in my hand
         and find

a shallow depression in the sand
   that was not a depression
      until the stone was lifted
         to reveal

a loneliness that was not mine
   until the water left
      and this stone sank
         into my hand

In a Winter Space

The neighbor's plastic geese fool me
    every time, but not because I think
them real, though they are realistic,
    for they lack a certain gooseness,

that wavelike walk, the feet that drop
    like ladies' handkerchiefs in old movies,
the flattened, suspicious eye. Still,
    the illusion holds that they might be geese,

that the decoy can attract the real thing,
    and the only fox I've ever seen is stalking
a plastic goose . . . eight below, twelve inches
    of snow, and hunger makes him believe,

makes it possible for me, too, to see
    the truth behind the illusion.
The rigid neck, the awkward stance, the sloping,
    gooselike body are all just right,

and in this breathless moment, almost as real
    as the fog that freezes about the fox's face,
and the doubt that holds us both, still
    wondering, in this winter space.

To the Power of the Air

along this ledge
some equation is playing itself out,

against the sill
small birds fall and rise again,

tracks, cosines and tangents
in the snow, explain the physics of flight

finite numbers tumble
toward infinity and everything is multiplied

by the power of the air

stunned by the glass, a dove
lies on the ledge until air finds its way

and wind, fingering his feathers,
whispers the equation that lifts him

off the ledge . . . into the air

unlike the sparrow
who froze before he could quicken

wings spread, eyes open

Not Understanding Hands

Not understanding   some things
require two hands   the dog despairs
when I lift my hand from her neck
to turn a page

her nose nuzzles my elbow
works its way   between my arm
and my body   and flips my hand
so it will fall   once again

across her neck   I grab
big fistfuls of skin and fur
I make mountains   down her spine
stroke the softness   of her knee

then move upward   pulling
her ears   palming her head
running   the furrow
between   her eyes

until   she melts   into a world
I have never known   a world
without hands   where the body waits
until feeling   alone

becomes knowledge   and thoughts
become   sensations
she accepts   all forms of giving
when she falls to the ground

I hear   the rush of air
the dull resonance   of earth
and bone   and my hand   lost
between her world   and mine   floats

Ropes and Ladders

The old dog we think too blind to know
barks at the door until her breath fogs
the glass and I, too, step outside to see

on one of those winter nights
when the sky and earth seem reversed.
Snow glitters beneath our feet,
the sky is black and starless, and deep

along the hedgerow, a small creature is digging,
raccoon or rabbit, impossible to know,
but warm and black and full of intent.

It is digging skyward, pushing through the roots
of stars, chewing at the webbing of the universe.
The only sound is the creak of the cold
as it tightens the lid on house and lawn.

We watch until my hands grow numb and the dog
lifts her feet to warm them in the night air.
I coax her to the door, help her up the stairs,

and we wander off to bed, traveling
through a damp and earthy darkness, climbing
the intricate ladder of sleep, as we grope
for a hold on some steep cliff, hearing

only the whimper of ropes and lines
and the swish of the wind, as time tangles
about our feet, and we awaken on the other side

of the day where everything is bright
and properly placed, and even the old dog
blinks, no more surprised than I, to find
everything familiar, so much the same.

Notes

"English 123 discusses Virginia Woolf"
Virginia Woolf committed suicide by filling her pockets
with stones and walking into the River Ouse.

"Watercolor"
Peter Spier won the Caldecott Medal for his picture book,
Noah's Ark. Paintings not included in the children's book hang in
various U.S. museums. The quotes are from a personal interview.

"On The Beach"
On the Beach, a novel by Nevil Shute, is about nuclear
holocaust. It was published in 1957. The movie starred Gregory
Peck and Ava Gardner.

Selected by Robert A Fink, *A Desk in the Elephant House* is the seventh winner of the Walt McDonald First-Book Competition in Poetry. The Competition is supported generously through donated subscriptions from *The American Scholar, The Atlantic Monthly, The Georgia Review, The Hudson Review, The Massachusetts Review, Poetry,* and *The Southern Review.*